The Jam Jar Lifeboat

and

Other Novelties Exposed

Poems by

Kay Ryan

Drawings by

Carl Dern

Red Berry Editions

2008

Poems © Kay Ryan 2008

Drawings © Carl Dern 2008

ISBN 978-0-9815781-1-8
Second Printing 2009

For permission to reprint any part of this book, write to
Red Berry Editions, Business Office,
1648 Ocean View Avenue, Kensington, California 94707.

Quotations from Believe It or Not! © 2008 Ripley
Entertainment Company
Believe It or Not!® is a registered trademark of
Ripley Entertainment, Inc.

Kay Ryan is Poet Laureate of the United States, 2008-2010.

Printed in Canada.

The Teutonic Amazon

Empress Elizabeth (1345–1393), wife of German
Emperor Charles IV, was so strong she could rip a suit
of steel armor from top to bottom with her bare hands.

Ripley's Believe It or Not!

This was more interesting to others
than to her. She appreciated
being able to open a stuck jar
or rehang a door when Charles
was off at one of his wars,
but what was tearing armor
good for? Really, there is
such a thing as excess strength,
strength beyond usefulness, strength you have
no business having. You can destroy things
just demonstrating.

THE JAM JAR LIFEBOAT

invented in 1831 by a man named Bateman who
insisted it was unsinkable, sank the first time it was tested.

Ripley's Believe It or Not!

It was quixotic to think
the cold grey North Atlantic
might be survived in a jam jar boat.
It is not enough that one of something
can be made to float with its lid sealed tight.
One rat might survive one night
on a single treadmill bottle
but even that would be a battle.
Bateman always hated how small truths
extrapolated so poorly. He came up with
really good small ones almost hourly.

LEOPOLD LOEWY

a chessmaster of Vienna, Austria, in the belief that it would keep him more fit for chess, never wore an overcoat in sixty-two years.

Ripley's Believe It or Not!

Many of the Loewy family
dressed even less warmly.
They reduced their layers
as they increased levels
of professional difficulty.
Leopold Loewy only had to be
ready for wars on flat boards
among figures of limited mobility.
His sister, Godiva, wrote poetry
and so wore no more than her long hair
if she went out to see anybody.

WHOOPEE

*The Mayor of Grand Lemps, France, issued an ordinance
that any inhabitant may enter a saloon and drink his fill and
then leave without paying. He was a prohibitionist.*

Ripley's Believe It or Not!

This would take care of the bistros in short order.
There would be no point purveying liquor.
All the little drink saucers
that stacked on zinc counters
would go back to the cupboard.
The cheap heavy-based glasses
would be used for bud vases.
The prostitutes pimps lowlife scoundrels
and tired worn-faced working people
and mustachioed *patron* in an apron
and bright-buttoned *gendarmes* and
peasants with their crates of chickens
and baskets of produce from their farms
would all just have to go home.

GUYAL VACA SEGUAL, FIRE EATER

*says in his letter to Mr. Ripley: 'I eat fire, play with
lead in my mouth. I take bath in gasoline and set myself in
fire. I step in red hot oven and roast pound of meat in same
to convince you and emerge cool as ice. I am King of Fire,
the whip of fire,' etc.*

Ripley's Believe It or Not!

It is redundant to have any more
than one of your accomplishments
Señor. When you have done what you said
about drinking hot lead, who could
want an encore? So many acts of self-immolation
call your methods into question.
You say these things are not tricks,
but why else would you take fire baths
or roast meat in your bare hands?
We must doubt people who stand
what there is no reason to stand.

CHANG

Chinese giant wrote his name on the
wall eleven feet above the floor.

Ripley's Believe It or Not!

Again and again
he wrote the
character for his name
high on walls,
well over door frames,
until no shop or temple
but said Chang, Chang!
far above eye level.

If he had been a
normal sized boy
he would have
been in trouble.
That boy of yours
is incorrigible,
the villagers
would have said.
They would not have
admired what he did.

And Chang did not admire
what he did. His brush work
was rather bad. Chang,
Chang, Chang, Chang, he wrote,
more bored than defiant,
hoping only to be
laughed at by a later giant.

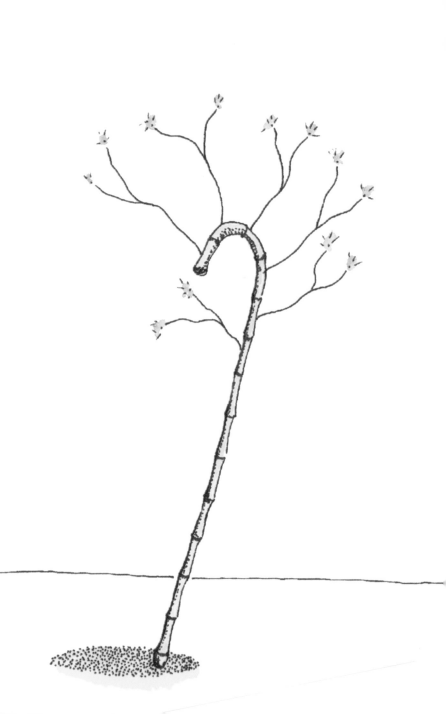

THE WALKING STICK INSECT

of South America often loses an antenna or leg—but always grows a new appendage. Often nature makes a mistake and a new antenna grows where the leg was lost.

Ripley's Believe It or Not!

Eventually the
most accident-prone
or war-weary
walking sticks
are entirely
reduced to antennae
with which they
pick their way
sensitively,
appalled by
everything's
intensity.

LOBSTER

Gerard de Nerval, Parisian poet and author, had a pet
lobster which he led through the streets of Paris on a leash.

Ripley's Believe It or Not!

It was eighteen fifty.
Clac-Clac was his name,
a pale salmon color, and dusty
from crossing the city
the way the city was then.

Every night his master
ate him and went for another,
whom he named Clac-Clac again.

"Even a lobster with his carapace
can't stand more than one turn
around this stinking circus,"
Nerval said with bitterness,

rigging himself and his lobster
up for today's appearance.

MURDER AT MIDNIGHT

*If everyone who was told about it told two other people
within twelve minutes, everybody on earth would know
about it before morning.*

Ripley's Believe It or Not!

But people would begin getting it
a little bit wrong. Long before daylight,
the *murder at midnight* would be
sugar stolen outright. The fate
of the dead man would not extend
beyond his gate. Only those
right now missing his little habits,
his footfall, his sleeping noises,
will know, and they can't really tell;
news doesn't really travel very well.

EMPEROR AGHA MOHAMMED KAHN
(1737–1797)

of Persia, was assassinated by two servants whom he had sentenced to death, but whom he had allowed to continue serving him while awaiting execution.

Ripley's Believe It or Not!

A less dense emperor
would know you never
postpone a sentence.
No matter how much
you need table help
or linen service,
these men have lost
their sense of allegiance.
Insults to your home
no longer strike them as personal.
The doomed can't feel the same
about your rooms, domes, or
Xanadu in general.

PERSONALITY

The word "personality" contains 1,307
other words.

Ripley's Believe It or Not!

At last count,
but surely it has
doubled since that.
Personality is invasive.
Allowed into a plot of language
it is more productive
than zucchini. Anyone
who cultivates personality
had better have neighbors
and imaginative recipes
because you are going to be
begging for relief
from your abundance.
You will come to know
it as a nuisance.

April 1, 570

Dear Ben,

I hope you enjoyed the little joke of the two—line piece.

Enclosed please find the remaining stanzas.

Best regards to the missus and happy April Fools Day.

Yours truly,
Anna

AMRA TARAFA

(544–570)

celebrated Arab poet, was buried alive by
order of Prince Amru Ben because the Prince
disliked a two-line epigram Tarafa wrote.

Ripley's Believe It or Not!

It takes so much to please,
so little to offend,
Amra Tarafa discovered
toward the end
of his short time
in the court of Amru Ben.
What worth, my thousand heavens,
my thousand fig gardens,
he asked himself as the mortar
hardened.

Two Noses

Bidault, a French peasant, had two noses.

Ripley's Believe It or Not!

But they were not
concurrent.
His baby nose
dropped off
and his adult nose
was revealed under it.
For a few days
he had to
breathe through his mouth,
but this simple story
has been altered
far beyond truth.

LADY'S WRIST WATCH

found by Mrs Jean Last in a sealed can of pears.
Hollesly, England, March, 1959

Ripley's Believe It or Not!

When they are there,
I eat pears, says Mrs Last,
who likes pears best
among the tinned fruits.
Friends and family
abuse me mercilessly
for my partiality to pears,
finding them innocuous
and vaguely gritty,
but I like to keep them on hand
in case of emergency (such as
the family one day all packing off
to the City, leaving me here in Hollesly,
thrown, as it were, to the wolves,
which, should it ever occur,
would be toast, lemon tea, and pear
after pear from the shelves).

FELIX AND ANTON STEINMEIER

identical twins, climbed Dachstein Peak
in Austria together 1,400 times.

Ripley's Believe It or Not!

After a while
nobody inquired
after the Steinmeier
twins. They were
off climbing Dachstein
Peak again.

Each time they swore
would be their last,
saying their dual
farewells to the rocks
and eidelweiss,
the place where they
shared their lunch.

Their delicious lunch
of bread, cheese,
and pickles, and coffee
from the thermos bottle,
followed by the bar
of chocolate they
always broke in two.

Each time they meant
to go down and lead
separate lives
but it was more than
they could do.